# Finding
# The
# Right Man

# Finding
# The
# Right Man

# Rom Wills
## Wills Publishing

# Finding The Right Man

Copyright 2003, 2012. 2014
by
Romuald P. Wills

ISBN-13 978-0692303245
ISBN-10 0692303243

# Table of Contents

# Introduction

Never say never.

In 1996 I wrote a pamphlet called *Finding a Good Man.* The pamphlet, which was only twelve pages long, was simply my thoughts at the time on how a woman could find a good man. I sold it for a dollar. In some cases I gave it away. To me it was my "two cents" on male/female relationships. I wasn't a PhD; I hadn't done any research. I didn't think the pamphlet would stack up against the numerous relationship books on the market.

Man, was I in for a surprise.

That little pamphlet, which I typed up and put together in my grandmother's living room, changed the direction of my life. I changed other people's lives as well. Women came back to me and said they needed to hear what I had to say. That pamphlet got me on cable TV and led to bigger things because so many men wanted something for them. I was prompted to write *Nice Guys and Players: Becoming the Man Women Want* and its follow-up, *Sexual*

*Chemistry, Nice Guys and Players Level II.* These two books have sold all over the world and I can honestly say that at least one copy of each of these books sells somewhere on the planet every single day.

Now life is funny. When I was pushing *Finding a Good Man* men wanted something for themselves so I produced two books for men. Now when I make appearances or do book signings I have women who will buy either *Nice Guys and Players* or *Sexual Chemistry* despite me telling them that the book is primarily for men. I have had more women get something out of the books than some men. Numerous women asked when I would write something for them.

I had said I wouldn't write anything else for women because in my view there are plenty of relationship books for women. Yet women are still looking for these types of books and are always the majority at relationship forums and seminars.

That's why I decided to write this book.

Despite the books, tapes, movies, seminars, and forums, there are an increasing number of single women. This is causing long-term relationship problems such as infidelity, loneliness, depression, single parent households, and whole list of related problems. Even women who are in relationships are not satisfied with their men.

Our community is suffering because men and women are not in productive relationships. I've addressed the issue from the male side with the *Nice Guys and Players* series. *Finding the Right Man* is addressed to women, although men can read it to get a perspective.

This book is about finding the Right Man from the prospective of a man. I've lived an interesting life. I have interacted with thousands of women of different ages, races,

8

nationalities, and economic backgrounds. After a while you start to see the same patterns. I'm not a PhD in sociology or some other discipline. My greatest qualification is that I'm a man. I know what other men are looking for. I am somebody who presents a realistic approach to finding the Right Man. In addition, at a point in this book I will provide a powerful secret which, when employed by a woman, will draw men to her like moths to a flame. I will provide hints to this secret throughout the book and it will be very important to read every single word because even when I provide the secret it still might not sink in unless seen in the context of the entire book. Everything in this book is meant to be applied in a holistic fashion. Everything works together.

As you read along don't think of this as a mere book. Think of it as a letter from one friend to another.

# Belief
## The Foundation for Finding the Right Man

The following article was written for an electronic newsletter I used to publish. This article provides a foundation for everything that follows in this book.

### The Power of Belief
### By
### Rom Wills

One thing never ceases to amaze me: the lack of faith people have when looking for a mate. In my life I have constantly encountered women who have expressed the belief that they could not find a man to share their life with. These women are usually professional, well-educated, and generally would make a good mate for some man. They just do not think they can find a good man on their "level". More about that "level" nonsense later. The thing that amazes me about these women is that many of them are long-time church members. Some even work in the church. My question has always been how can a woman claim to have faith in God and not use this same faith to believe she will find a good mate?

I am going to let everybody in on a secret. I have written before that I had a few secrets that allowed me to date a variety of women. One of the things that allowed me to do this was that I believed I could. I never looked at a woman I had a desire for and believed she would reject me. My belief has always been that if I could talk with a woman for at least a half-hour she would find me attractive. This might not have been necessarily true but I believed it and that made it true in my mind. By believing this I programmed my subconscious into putting out attractive energy, which drew women to me and caused them to behave according to my beliefs. My beliefs quite literally created a reality. I learned about the power of belief by growing up in a very spiritual family. I learned that through God all things are possible.

I have encountered many so-called educated and religious women who are in pain because of their negative relationships. How can they say they believe in God and have trouble finding a mate?

The reason is that they believe that they will not find a good man. For example, Jane believes that all men are abusive cheaters and that there are no good men. She always ends up in relationships with bad men. She's blaming the men but she is the cause of her problems. By believing all men are bad her spirit will act on that belief and send attractive energy out to those men. That is her reality. Jane may encounter good men all the time but because of her beliefs they will not register on her radar. Once Jane starts believing that there are good men, and that they are available, her subconscious will change to attract those men.

If this example is too deep for people let's look at it another way. Haven't we all seen those women even the bad men respect? I have met quite a few of these women and they had one thing in common: they saw the good in the men they encountered. Their energy actually caused the men in their environment to change. I remember one time I was in a store ran by some Muslim sisters. They were very peaceful and when I left I realized how my reaction to them was different from my reaction to other women. Their behavior made me feel more peaceful and agreeable. These women could have sold anything to me at that moment. Women who believe that good men exist will attract the good ones and bring out the good in the bad ones. Once again this comes down to faith.

## IF THE WOMEN WHO SAY THEY CANNOT FIND A GOOD MAN START TO BELIEVE THAT THEY CAN, THEY WILL!

Let me share a true story with you. My sister is mentally disabled. Back in the beginning of 1995 she began to say she wanted a computer. Nobody in the family could afford one even with credit cards. My sister's tested IQ is around 60. She can pray though. She prayed and asked for that computer everyday for a year. She NEVER wavered. She NEVER believed that she wouldn't get that computer. On Christmas Day 1995, my sister opened the box containing her new computer AND the box containing a 600 dollar laser printer. She got what she wanted because of her faith in God. The same principle can be applied to any sincere need in life.

If a mentally disabled person can have strong faith in something why not so-called educated women? How can they believe that God will provide them with material goods and not a mate?

Men and women can change their lives by simply believing they can. If someone truly believes in God then they should realize that with the power of belief all things are possible.

\*\*\*\*\*\*\*\*\*\*\*\*\*\*

I started with this article to make ladies think as they go along. Every single word in this book is useless if you do not have the power of belief. A woman has to believe she can find the Right Man. If you don't believe, all the following information is useless.

**What's the point of looking for a good man if you don't believe you can find one?**

# The Choice

The following is a quote from my book, **Nice Guys and Players - Becoming The Man Women Want:**

One day, a friend of mine I'll call Jim decided to tell me the secret of his success with women. Jim attracted women like manure attracts flies. Women would quite literally camp out on his front lawn to see him and it wasn't even his house. He lived with his mother until he got married. Jim wasn't rich. He didn't have his own car. Jim would have women chase after him. The irony was you could never call him a player. I have known him since we were ten and I have never heard him use a pickup line with a woman. Not once. My success with women when I was young was never anywhere near his. So one day, after I got him sufficiently drunk, Jim decided to tell me the secret of his success with women. After he told me I asked, "That's it?" Jim replied, "Yeah, that's it. Gimme another beer." Just like that I knew the answer. Of course

15

it took me a couple of years to master the concept, but hopefully it will take you a couple of weeks.

What's the secret? The secret is simple. **Women choose the men.** Sounds simple doesn't it? Well it is simple. Remembering those four words will get you more dating choices than you can handle. Mastering the concept behind those words will save you time, money, and heartbreak. The only time you will be without companionship is when you don't feel like being bothered. Women, in most cases, know exactly what they want in a man. They don't always end up with the men they want, but they still know. Women know who can turn them on and who cannot. Many women have told me they can take one look at a man and know whether or not they will date him. If a woman doesn't **choose** a man there is nothing he can do to win her heart. All the money, looks, prestige, charm, or power will not change her mind. Nice Guys and Players Pages 17 -19

**************

This is what I told the men but there is something here for the women. All ladies have to realize they have the power. In my observation there are three types of women: those who realize they choose the men and act accordingly; those who realize they choose but pretend like they don't; and those who have no idea about the power they possess.

In finding the Right Man, women have to take responsibility. They have to realize they have a choice and also a responsibility to themselves to choose correctly. If a woman makes the wrong choice, she has to take responsibility. For example,

Doris is a woman who consistently ends up with losers. These men never have anything going for them. Doris always wonders why these men are losers and why the men will not do anything to better themselves. The mistake Doris is making is that she is looking in the wrong direction. Instead of wondering why these men are losers she needs to look in the mirror and wonder why she is consistently choosing the same type of man over and over.

A woman choosing the man is only half the equation. The man must accept the choice. This book will provide the tools a woman can employ so that when she chooses a man he will choose her back.

Women need to make the right choice. Too many women make a choice and the man accepts and then later the woman finds out she made the wrong choice. The wrong choice can haunt a woman for the rest of her life.

# Self-Examination

Before a woman sets out to find the Right Man she has to work on herself. For example, Gina has met a man who has everything she wants in Dexter. Dexter is tall, handsome, well-built, financially successful, charismatic, and believes in monogamy. Yes ladies, men like this do exist. Gina is excited and thinks she has struck gold. Hold-up now. Dexter doesn't have an interest in Gina beyond friendship. Gina wonders why Dexter isn't interested. She thinks she's a great catch. Not in Dexter's eyes. He sees an out of shape, low self-esteem, and minimum wage earning woman who doesn't have plans for the future.

Sounds far-fetched? Not at all. Over the years I have encountered plenty of women who thought they were the bomb but in the eyes of men they weren't anything. This has even been the case when the woman was physically attractive, successful, educated, and on paper had everything going for her. But some men looking at the same woman may see something different and reject her. Many ladies get mad and wonder what's wrong with the men. Instead of focusing on the men, women need to look at themselves.

Not to seem like I'm picking on women I'll use myself as an example. I remember an interesting incident years ago with a young lady I'll call Elaine. I was interested in Elaine and she returned the feelings. I thought she was interested in me because of my looks, my education, my intelligence, and my finances. Elaine told me differently. She said she liked me because I ran errands for my grandmother and worked with kids. Another incident a few years later involved a young lady I'll call Dana. Dana kept me in a platonic mode. She had already admitted she had some attraction to me so I couldn't figure out why she didn't want to take it further. Then one day we were talking on the phone and I was trashing her profession. She responded, "Why do you think I'll sleep with you when you keep talking about my profession?" Man that woke me up. I considered it a valuable lesson. Despite what I had going for me I was lacking in area that was important to Dana. Many women make this same mistake. They think they are the bomb but are lacking in an area important to a particular man.

All women need to engage in serious self-examination before looking for the Right Man. In some cases this might mean professional help. Don't be afraid to see a therapist or any other health-care professional. Many women have baggage that goes back as far as childhood. That baggage, in many cases, will interfere with your pursuit of happiness. You have to unload that baggage as best as possible. If you don't want to see a mental health professional then talk to a minister, an elder, or even your best friend. Do whatever it takes to heal yourself of any emotional scars.

One mistake many women make is that they say they have their act together. This is the height of arrogance. Most women base this assertion on having a job, some education, and a nice place to live. Yet these same women are either without men or treated like sex objects. Every single person on this planet has growing to do. Ladies, unless you can walk on water and raise the dead, you do not have your act together and you need to focus on continual growth.

A woman must be willing to look at herself realistically in order to make the necessary changes for growth.

# Categories of Women

As I've stated, a woman may think she is the bomb while a man thinks she's a dud. You need to get an understanding of how men view the women they encounter. Men generally look at women in three general ways. A man will see a woman as a Friend, a Sex Partner, or Ms. Right. Part of self-examination is trying to get an idea of how men look at you, and, in the case of two of the categories, improve your behavior become more appealing.

## The Friend

This is the woman a man may share himself with emotionally, hang out with, be best buddies with, but will only be platonic with her. This can be a problem if the woman feels her buddy is the Right Man. Platonic friendship is a good thing. A woman, however, needs to examine why a man would only see her this way especially since men only tend to be voluntarily platonic with women they don't find attractive.

In some cases a man might marry this woman but would fool around or even leave once a more appealing woman comes into the picture.

If you're a woman who is consistently a friend and not a lover the issue is that you may not be sexually appealing to these men. A woman in the friend category needs to work on her sex appeal.

### Sex Partner

This is self-explanatory. No matter what this woman has going for her, this woman will never be seen as a serious mate by most men. Many women fall into this category. These women will draw a lot of attention because there is something about them that says while they would make a good sex partner they would not be considered Ms. Right.

A man is not going to involve this type of woman in his regular life. He will, as much as possible, try to limit his interactions with her to sex. He is not going to be interested in taking her out on the town or even introducing her to his friends. She will probably never meet his family unless it's by accident.

Sex partners are across the socio-economic spectrum. A professional woman is just as likely to be a sex partner as a welfare recipient. There are no boundaries with regard to sex.

A woman needs to be seen as more than a sex partner in order to find the Right Man.

## Ms. Right

This is the woman who everything going for her in a man's eyes. This is the woman who will settle down a player. Ms. Right is generally the woman who combines the best qualities of the Friend and the Sex Partner. Many men say they want a lady in public and a freak in the bedroom. This crude analogy pretty much sums it up. Men want that best buddy who can also satisfy them physically.

The goal of all women should be to grow to point where they become a Ms. Right in the eyes of not only one man but of several men.

# Keys to Becoming Ms. Right

## A. Physical Appearance

Ladies, let's face it. Men are visual. We are attracted to women because of physical appearance. We are made that way and no amount of political correctness and intellectualism will change that. You can be the nicest, most intelligent, most supportive person in the world but most men will not try to find out if you are out of shape, dress poorly, and in general do not take care of your physical appearance.

Ladies, exercise your body. A funny thing is that many women will get their hair done, wear fake hair, wear tons of make-up, get fake nails, and feel like men should be attracted to them. Ladies, I'm going to let you in on a secret: when we talk about women it's rare we talk about their hair, make-up, and nails in a positive sense. If we do, it's usually in the sense that the hair, make-up, and nails detract from a woman's appearance.

Ladies, we like bodies. We talk about bodies. The stair climber at the gym will do more for you than the hair dryer. More time in the gym and less in the nail salon will do wonders for attracting men to you.

As far as working out, all women should work to be in the best shape possible for their body type. If you are a larger woman, still work out but don't try to get skinny if it would hurt your body. Everybody is not meant to be size 2. There was a time when size 12-16 women caught my attention the quickest. Work with what you have.

Women should be cognizant of how they dress. Men are attracted to women with nice bodies wearing provocative clothing but they are typically going to be looking at them as sex partners. Women should work to express their sensuality without going overboard. A balance must be found between sexually provocative and tasteful.

Taking care of your health is very important. Substance abuse will detract from your appearance. Even cigarette smoking and alcohol will affect your appearance. I'm not saying don't smoke or drink but keep in mind that this will affect your appearance. If you are having trouble attracting a man you need to think about these things.

## B. Mental Attitude

One of the most amazing things I have encountered in my life is when I meet women who dog out men and yet want to find a good man. Women lose out on finding the Right Man simply because they have a bad attitude. Why would a man trying to accomplish something in life want a woman with a foul attitude, especially when he has a choice? Women may choose the men but the men must accept the choice.

A woman must develop herself mentally. Consider an observation made in the bookselling industry. Women tend to buy primarily fiction books such as romance novels while men tend to buy non-fiction. More women need to read non-fiction, other than relationship books, in an effort to better relate to men. This doesn't mean they should stop reading fiction but simply add to their reading list. You will also be contributing to your mental and spiritual growth.

Many women try to impress a man by telling him how independent she is. This actually pushes many men away. Most men want a woman who is independent but not to the extent she doesn't need him. Ladies, men and women need each other. Otherwise it would be pointless to even try to get together. Many women lose out by projecting this attitude. Basically you are telling the man you don't need him. Ask yourself this: if you don't need a man why should he spend his time and energy with you? All people want to feel important to their mates and potential mates.

From my point of view, and that of many men, I'm not sure how many women are truly independent anyway. I have personally observed many so-called independent women change their tune in a hurry as soon as they met an attractive man. Many men have complained about how their "independent women" changed into "dependent women" as the relationship progressed.

The thing that hurts women more than anything is seeing men in a negative light. Think back to what I said about power of belief. A woman who believes men are no good will only attract

26

those types of men. A woman who sees the good in men will attract good men.

Why should a man deal with a woman with a bad attitude? A strong positive man is going to have plenty of choices for a mate. That's reality. Why should a man deal with a woman who has a negative attitude, regardless of her physical appearance, when there are other women of equal attractiveness who are pleasant towards him?

# Unproductive Behavior

Many women fail to find the right man because they engage in behavior which causes them to lose out on a good man. Unproductive behavior comes in three general forms: Infidelity, Game Playing, and Exhibiting Masculine Behavior.

## A. Infidelity

Yeah ladies, I'm going there. Much is made about how men fool around on their wives and how men are dogs. Very few people focus on the women these men are fooling around with. These women want the Right Man but they are caught up with someone else's Right Man. These same women have the nerve to want a positive man in their lives.

A woman looking for the Right Man needs to avoid being the other woman. The women who don't know they are the other woman are excused until they find out. Many other women knowingly get involved with attached men. This behavior prevents a woman from finding the Right Man. How is she going to find the Right Man if she is involved with some other woman's man? Even if the man leaves his woman for you how long will it be before he leaves you for another woman?

On the other side of the coin you have women with two and three men. They have a different man for each occasion. If a woman wants to lead this type of lifestyle that's on her but if she wants the Right Man she needs to focus on one man. A woman with multiple partners is going to have trouble finding the Right Man. The reason is because the Right Man has too much going for him to be a part of a harem. Even if he does become a part of the harem you have to wonder how serious he is about you. If he knows you are with other men he is not going to see you as marriage material. A man wants a woman who is going to be faithful.

A major concern with men is whether their women will be faithful. If a woman is cheating on her man or running around with multiple sex partners a man is going to take this into consideration. A popular saying is that you can't turn a hoe into a housewife. Most men live by this. If a woman is behaving like a hoe she shouldn't expect to find the Right Man without telling lies. This leads to another problem: dishonesty.

Many women say they want honesty out of a man but do not manifest this character trait themselves. A law of the universe is that like attracts like. A dishonest woman will attract a dishonest man. Instead of happiness the result will be disappointment.

A woman looking for the Right Man must stop being the other woman. She also needs to stop having a different man for different occasions. The time spent hanging with different men can be better spent developing herself into Ms. Right.

### B. Game Playing

Many women complain about the games men play. I have a problem with that. In most cases, women see right through a man's games. There are very few men slick enough to truly pull the wool over a woman's eyes. Let's be honest here. Many women see through the games but choose to play along anyway. It takes two to play a game, so even if a man is trying to run game the woman doesn't have to play along. Some men are knuckleheads anyway. The woman, on her part, needs to come correct.

Some women start off playing games. There's that dishonesty thing again. This is stupid. A man with something going for himself does not have to put up with anything. A man has plenty of women to choose from. Unless he simply wants sex he's not going to put up with a game player.

A woman who's into playing games needs to do self-examination to determine why she feels the need to play games or even participate in a man's games. Relationships are serious business.

### C. Exhibiting Masculine Traits

One thing that most men find undesirable is a woman who behaves in a masculine manner and yet wants a mate. Men are attracted to feminine energy. Feminine energy is softer, receptive, cooperative, and peaceful. Masculine energy is assertive, protective,

30

and aggressive. Feminine energy is very powerful in terms of attracting men.

A powerful universal law is of polarity which, in essence, states that opposites do indeed attract. Think about two magnets. For them to attach you need a plus side and a negative side. Two plus magnets will not attach and two negative magnets will not attach. This same principle is at work in male-female relationships. A man who is exhibiting masculine energy will be repelled by a woman who is exhibiting the same type of energy. This man, however, will be drawn to a woman exhibiting feminine energy. Sounds simple? Apparently not judging from observations in the community. What's been happening is that there are an increasing number of women who are expressing masculine traits and in some cases starting to look more masculine. The causes behind this are complex and will quite frankly take a few volumes to explore. What is more of a concern here is to recognize the issue and provide a solution. Women need to focus on consciously expressing their inner feminine energy.

In general, men are attracted to women primarily because they represent what men are not. For example, Ted is a muscular man who is very assertive and on the go. He's always into something. His lady Claire is more passive with a softer body. She is more the homebody. She has a calming effect on Ted. That's because she adds the element of peace to his life. He doesn't need somebody who's assertive with hot energy like he has. This is a key aspect in male/female relationships that few people talk about. Relationships work best when both parties bring traits that complement each other. If both people have the same traits the relationship will not grow because growth only occurs when there is something to contrast with.

The bottom line is that a heterosexual man is not going to be attracted to a woman who for all intents and purposes is expressing masculine energy. She will tend to attract effeminate men. A woman must consciously avoid expressing masculine energy in order to attract the Right Man.

# Compatibility

A major issue with a woman finding the Right Man is simply finding someone to who is compatible to her. In the media, public forums, and private settings one of the biggest concerns women have is finding someone with whom they can truly relate. They have trouble finding someone on their level.

I want to address that "level" issue. I have met many women who claim they cannot find a man on their level. Most of the time they are talking about their income and educational level. First of all, money DOES NOT give a person character and personality. There are plenty of evil people with money and no love in their lives. Secondly, many women believe that just because they have two or three degrees they are above somebody. Degrees do not mean you are intelligent. They only mean you can remember what somebody TRAINED you to do. Before somebody thinks I hate people with degrees, please know that I have both college and law degrees. Those degrees, however, do not make me a better person. How I treat people is more important. My REAL education came from my family and living in the real world. Too many women with degrees look down on men without degrees. These same women wonder why they are alone. They are alone because they think a law degree or an MBA can take the place of a PhD in common sense. This goes for men as well as women. People need to stop thinking that some piece of paper or economic status makes them better than another human being.

Educational and economic status is easily changed. Stop worrying about a man's financial portfolio. Pay enough attention to make sure he isn't irresponsible but make sure the man is trying to do something positive with his life. A man with bad credit doesn't mean he is bad. Find out why he has bad credit. Things happen to people. He could have had a failed business, school loans, a medical emergency, anything. Don't hold his past against him. Judge the man for who he is now and where he is going.

One thing to consider is that even if two people have the same educational and economic status they still may not be compatible. For example, John and Kelly both have dual degrees and have jobs paying six figures. On the surface it would seem like they would be compatible. Hold on, wait a minute. Education and money are only two superficial qualities. John and Kelly have two entirely different outlooks on life based on their backgrounds. John grew up on welfare and feels it's his obligation to give back to the community. Despite his education and money he lives a modest lifestyle and gives a lot of his time and energy to community service. Kelly on the other hand grew up in an upper middle class environment and is very materialistic and self-absorbed. John and Kelly have nothing in common beyond their shared status.

Now the woman reading this may see the above example as common sense but is it really? Often in the media and in private circles, women, particularly professional women, will talk about what they want in a man. The qualities listed are usually superficial such as education and status. Many women will encounter these types of men, date them, and still find that they are not satisfied. The reason they are not satisfied is that their criteria was superficial.

Ladies, allow me to share a secret with you for finding a truly compatible mate. Do not look for a man who is compatible with your profession, economic status, and even religion. Look for a man who is compatible with your dreams. That corporate 9 to 5 person isn't the real you. Find someone who is compatible with the real you.

People generally have two faces. Co-workers and associates see a public one. The private one is the one seen by family members and lovers. Most people evaluate a mate based on their public face and their credentials. This is a big mistake. Ask yourself this question: When you strip away the degrees, the money, the dates, can you deal with this person? That should be the only criteria. When two people are intimate, they open up their truest selves to each other. Those external trappings mean nothing. It doesn't matter if you have three degrees, your own home, and a late model car. It doesn't matter what your stock portfolio looks like. When you're dealing intimately with a man that connection is soul to soul. All those props mean absolutely nothing at that point. The connection with a man must be at a spiritual level or else it's doomed to failure.

One issue regarding compatibility is that some women try to mold a man into the man of their dreams. Women must resist this urge at all costs. For a woman to do this is an act of selfishness. You can't turn a handyman into an office worker. You can't turn an office worker into an entrepreneur. Every person must ultimately follow his or her own path. You cannot force a man to follow the path in your mind. You can't force someone to conform to your needs. The best you can hope for is that the man is naturally compatible to your true self. It doesn't have to be a perfect fit because there is always room for growth. He just needs to be going in the same general direction as you are. Ultimately the best way to get a man is to let him be himself to the extent it doesn't cause you harm.

Women should look for someone with whom they can grow. Don't think you or your man will stay the same. When looking for somebody to grow with look for somebody who actually growing. To find a loser who is doing nothing with his life and expect him to grow may be an unrealistic expectation. Look for someone actively trying to grow.

The key thing to remember is to look for someone compatible with your true self and someone who is actively trying to grow on their own.

# Romantic Illusions

One of the biggest obstacles to a woman finding the Right Man is that her criteria are based on her own romantic ideals. For example, Jennifer's ideal mate is one who takes her to expensive restaurants, the latest plays, gives her flowers, gifts, cards, and enjoys romantic getaways. Not bad things. Romance such as this is needed in a relationship. It adds the necessary spice. The problem with Jennifer is that she expects a man to do this ALL the time. Don't laugh, we all know women who are like this. As soon as the romance slacks off with a particular man Jennifer dumps him. The problem is that she is too caught up in the excitement of romantic illusions. These romantic illusions are detrimental to mature relationships.

Women have to let go of romantic notions if they really want a man. Too many women want the fairy tale but then become disappointed when the man doesn't live up to their fantasy. I have observed and talked with many women about why they have rejected particular men. The vast majority rejected men not on character issues but on things like not bringing flowers at a certain time, not being able to afford dinner at a five star restaurant, etc, etc. Romantic outings are definitely needed in the relationship but let's get real, they are no reason to break up. Yet many women do so.

Many women lose out on very good men because they are chasing romantic fantasies. They are so busy looking for Mr. Goodbar that they miss the perfect man for them who may be less than ideal romantically. There's a price to pay for women who get caught in romantic illusions. These women are the ones who take a beating emotionally by a particular class of men. These men know how to push a woman's romantic buttons and thus have their way with her. This wouldn't be the case if women didn't put as big an emphasis on romance.

This is not to say that romance isn't important it's just that overindulgence in it can have devastating consequences. There must be a balance between romance and practicality.

Women under the influence of romantic illusions are guilty of using faulty criteria for choosing a mate. They are looking for that knight in shining armor. Only a few men will fit her criteria. There are two groups of men as a result. There is the select group and the non-select group. The men in the select group are the ones who can play to a woman's romantic illusions. The men in the non-select group are the ones who cannot meet a woman's romantic expectations.

Once women let go of romantic illusions, they will find that the group of men they find attractive will gradually expand. All of a sudden, that short, hardworking man with glasses, and a little pudgy, goes from a man you would have ignored previously to someone whose company you would now enjoy. A pudgy man can always hit the gym. A woman who is looking for a man who is 6'2" will find that she can be just as happy with a man who is 5'9", especially if she is 5'3".

Men are not going to be romantic all the time or even most of the time. There are going to be times when the man is down. There are going to be times when he is tired. There are going to be times when he isn't exciting. Life has its up and downs. Think about it like this, those romantic evenings where you get flowers, dinner, a play, and a sensuous nightcap generally take money. Even if the man entertains you at his home he still has to buy the food. The man had to work for this money and most men have to put up with a lot of crap on their jobs and probably more if they own a business. A hardworking man is going to be too tired sometimes to even think about romance. A lady reading this may think this should be obvious but I don't think so. I've talked to many women, men, and even divorce attorneys. Many women are so caught up in romantic illusions that the minute the men are anything less than romantic they are ready to kick them to the curb.

The bottom line is that a woman looking for the Right Man needs to take the romantic illusions out of the equation. You don't have to let him off the hook totally. A man needs to provide some level of romance but a woman cannot get too caught up in the romance being provided. There must always be a balance.

# Sexual Chemistry

I will now discuss the secrets to generating sexual chemistry with a man. Men are moved to great heights when stimulated by sex. Many people consider men to be sex-obsessed but then do not ask why they are this way. Men who are truly successful in life have one thing in common: they have found a constructive use for their sex drive. A woman's ability to arouse a man is the key to this sex drive. The woman who can keep her man aroused will have two things. One, a man who will have the drive to succeed in any chosen endeavor. Two, she will have a man predisposed to being monogamous. The biggest single reason men fool around is for sex. Two of the best ways to keep a man from cheating is to keep him aroused and focused on a project.

The whole sex thing isn't just about pleasing a man anyway. Too many women don't enjoy sex for its own sake. Too many see it as an obligation. Even many women who do enjoy sex are not satisfied because the men are not fulfilling their needs.    What follows are the keys to developing sexual chemistry with a man. When a woman can truly arouse a man she not only satisfies him but she will find that he will be more motivated to satisfy her needs.

### Keys to Sexual Chemistry

### A.  Physical appearance

A key component to generating sexual chemistry with a man is physical appearance.   A man's nature is to be attracted to a woman based on her physical appearance.    No amount of intellectualism or political correctness will change this.    The Creator made us this way for a reason.    Now a mature man will also check out a woman's emotional and spiritual traits but this will generally occur after he gets past the initial physical attraction.   The physical is what draws a man to a woman.  You can be the most sweetest, loving, loyal woman in the world and the man will not be inclined to find out about your personality if he doesn't think you have a nice body.    Even if somehow you do meet, if he doesn't find you physically attractive you will be in the "Friend" category.

The key to a woman developing her physical appearance is to engage in some type of exercise program, particularly programs which will tone her muscles and also keep access fat off her stomach.   Fat around the stomach area is key.   The ideal shape for a woman is an hourglass figure.   There should a contrast between the breasts, the waists and the hips.   For example, Suzanne is a woman who is 5'10" and 200 pounds yet men fall all over themselves to be with her.   The reason is that despite her weight she has a relatively small waist and flat stomach. It's the SHAPE that's most important. I know many woman get caught into trying to be a size 6 or below but the reality is that it's not genetically possible for all women to be that size or even desirable for many men. There are many men who prefer women who are size 12 and up. The key is the shape and not the clothes size.

In addition to exercises which deal with access weight around the stomach, a woman may want to spend time working on exercises which strengthen and tone her legs and butt. Even though there seems to be an emphasis on a woman's breasts in the media many men are attracted to a nice booty and legs.

Ultimately you want to be in the best shape possible. This will do more to attract a man than degrees or material possessions.


## B. Clothing

A woman can have a body that will put a man into a trance and cause a few accidents but it would be irrelevant if she covers it too much or doesn't wear clothes that enhance her figure. There are two considerations with the clothes a woman wears. One, does the clothing enhance her physical appearance and two, are the clothes feminine?

Once the woman has improved her physical appearance the clothing she chooses to wear will either shield that appearance or magnify it. For example, Charlene despite having a "coke bottle" figure wears very loose clothing that effectively hides her body. So when men see her they are not inclined to approach her regardless of her signals because they don't see her figure and thus are not aroused. She isn't able to generate sexual chemistry with them.

On the other hand Kyra has the same type of figure but she doesn't have a problem generating sexual chemistry because she will wear tight tops, shorter than average skirts, and four-inch pumps. Even in business attire she will dress provocatively. As a result men fall over themselves to talk with her.

In the two examples above the women are wearing clothes which project two aspects of femininity: maternal and sensual. One issue I'm seeing more and more is women dressing like men. It's very important that a woman looking for the Right Man doesn't dress like one. If she has a "coke bottle" figure but wears clothes like a man she is not going to generate sexual chemistry with the men in her environment.

The key to understanding with clothes is that they magnify a person's body. It's very important that women are cognizant of how they choose and wear their clothing. Using the examples from above, Charlene is in a sense neutralizing her physical appearance by covering up her body. The average man will view her as a friend. Kyra on the other hand is over-magnifying her body. The average man will see her as a sex partner. The key once again is balance.

The clothing women wear should strike a balance between sensual and maternal. A woman wants to dress sensual enough to draw the man's attention. Instead of four inch pumps maybe one-inch pumps. Instead of a real short mini skirt maybe a skirt that stops maybe an inch above the knees. Trust me, this will still get the man's attention but at the same time he will not be as focused on simply physical gratification. He will be more amenable to the woman's emotional/spiritual traits.

## C. Attitude

We've all seen women who have great bodies and have something going on mentally. Yet these women still have problems finding the Right Man and generating sexual chemistry. For example, Susan has a great body and is very intelligent. Men usually see her initially as a sex partner and then as a friend if they feel like dealing with her. She's never a Ms. Right despite what she has going for her. The problem is that she has a poor attitude towards men. She is very defensive towards men which shows in her tone of voice and body language. Despite an initial attraction men are turned off by her mannerisms.

A woman's attitude toward men is very important in generating sexual chemistry. In a nutshell she needs to like men. Many women despite wanting a man do not like men. Many women are defensive as a result. If a man approaches them their defensiveness will turn the man off. Many men will not even approach.

Ladies, here's a powerful secret in attracting the right man to you: practice being receptive. One of the biggest reasons why many women are not approached by men is that they are simply too defensive. Some defensiveness is necessary as a protection against some of the less evolved men out there. Sometimes though women are defensive in friendlier environments which may cause them to lose out on a good man because their body language tells a man to stay away.

Even when the man and woman have sex a receptive attitude is needed. If the woman is defensive she will not enjoy sex with the man. During sex the woman is receiving from the man.

44

Her actions during sex should reflect this. She should be like a placid lake that is being stirred by a storm. She should allow the man to stir her up. If she is defensive he will not be able to do his job and as a result she will tend to build up tension that will not be released by an orgasm. One of the biggest reasons women don't have orgasms is that they are too defensive as a result of their attitudes towards men.

A woman looking for the Right Man needs to examine her attitude towards men. A poor attitude will lead to poor sexual chemistry.

### A Final Note about Sexual Chemistry

Ladies, whether you are going through the steps to develop sexual chemistry or you already have them, please do not use sexuality as a tool to control a man. Sex shouldn't be about power. Sex is about two souls coming together whether it's pure lust or pure love. Whatever the case, it's about SHARING. Too many women use sex as a tool to control the men in their lives. If a woman has to resort to sex to control a man she does not have the Right Man. The Right Man will be in your life because he wants to be and not because you exercise some type of control over him.

On the other hand do not allow yourself to be controlled or used sexually. You want a man to respect your entire being and not simply see you as a sex partner. You may feel like that man is the right one but you still need to set boundaries. Do not want a man so badly that you compromise your principles. If you feel you need to get to know a man for a few weeks, or months, before sleeping with him, stick to that. It's very important that he

45

respects you. The vast majority of men want a woman they can respect.

# What to Look for in the Right Man

I've talked with literally thousands of women about what they look for in men. The overwhelming majority will say things like certain looks, height, education level, religion, income, neighborhoods, and cars. I've even scanned personal ads to see what women are looking for. After doing this research and reading books by other people I came to the conclusion that the reason why so many women have trouble finding the Right Man is that quite frankly they don't know what to look for in a man. Many women will find exactly what they say they want and still not be satisfied.

I'm going to present what a woman needs to look for in a man. I'm saying this because I know women want the best type of man they can find but they are not going to find this because the criteria being used is very faulty. Women need to be looking for two things in a man: character and purpose.

## Character

Women should always look for a man with character. Before defining character I want to distinguish it from honesty. Many women will say they want honesty in a man but an honest man may not necessarily have a good character. Honesty doesn't mean ethical. A man calling you ugly is being honest if that's how he feels. A man telling you he has six other women is being honest. A man who tells you he lives a life of crime is being honest with you. Women need to take it a step further and look for a man of character, of principles, of discipline.

Now many women will say that they look for a man of principles. Do they? Is a woman looking for a man of principles when she cheats with a married man? Is a woman looking for a man of principles when she is looking for money from a man? Is she looking for a man of principles when she has two or three men she's seeing at the same time? The answer to all of these questions is a resounding NO! First of all a man of character is typically not going to be a cheater. A man of character is not going to play the money game. A man of character is not going to be part of a harem. So how do I define character?

Character is about going through life with a code of conduct that provides a standard of behavior that a man will follow. This code may come from a holy book or something he developed from within. This is the Christian man who lives by what Jesus taught and doesn't deviate from the teachings when it's convenient. He follows this code regardless of the circumstances. This is the martial artist who lives by the code of only using his skills for self-defense regardless of the situation. This is the man who believes in

48

monogamy and doesn't stray even when the opportunity presents itself. It's the man who lives by his word. The man with character is not a hypocrite. He doesn't say one thing and do the other. The man with character is the one who, when he does stray from his ideals because he still human, is able to correct the situation and face the consequences of any transgression.

The man with character is the one who is willing, by his words and actions, to rise above the herd even if he has to go against the tide. He stands for what's right.

## Purpose

The second thing a woman needs to look for in a man is someone who is either living their life purpose or is at least in the process of finding his purpose. I would be rich if I had a dime for every time I had a conversation with a woman who complained about her man. Through all of this I found one interesting thing. The women were dealing with men who weren't doing anything with their lives. When I say the men weren't doing anything with their lives I don't mean they were lazy, unemployed bums. These men typically had education and jobs. Many were professionals. The issue was that these men only worked and partied. These men didn't have a greater meaning to their lives.

Ladies, let me tell you something. The worst type of man is the one without a sense of purpose to his life. This is regardless of whether he's a lazy bum or making six figures. This is the man who will cheat on you the quickest. This is the man who will treat you like a sex partner. This is the man you will have an empty relationship with once you get past the romantic illusions. Many women get caught up in a man's degrees and money until they take a closer look and see that's all there is to him. In reality this man will not let you get close to him because he realizes that once you see past his mask you will see him as a fraud.

On the other hand you have a man with a purpose. For example, Kevin is a man whose dream is to build an independent school for at risk African-American children. He will only deal with positive women who will not cause him to be distracted from his life purpose. A woman in a relationship with him will find that Kevin doesn't have time to play games or cheat or deal with a woman only as a sex partner. A man with a purpose realizes that he needs the right woman to help him accomplish his mission and in turn he can help her to accomplish her mission. A man focused on something is not going to let anyone distract him. If you find a man who consistently doesn't do right you will find a man who doesn't have a purpose to his life.

A man of character and purpose is the type of man a woman needs to pursue. Now there's not a lot a men out there like this but if women start looking for men with character and purpose, men will react accordingly. Men will work on their character and search for their purpose. Men run game, flash money, get big cars, and tell lies because this is what they see women respond to. Men do what they believe works. If women stopped looking for the superficial things and looked for men with character, men would change in a hurry. It starts with women and their choices.

For the woman reading this you need to do two things. One, you need to reevaluate your criteria for choosing a man. Two, start looking for men with character and a sense of purpose.

For women, who already look for these things quite frankly you need to be more vocal about it. All men hear about are women looking for status and money. Men can only go by what you say.

# What Men Look for

No matter how much a woman improves herself she still needs to understand what men look for in a woman. Women may choose the man but the man has to choose them back. Refer back to what I said about how men categorize women. When we see a woman we usually see a "sex partner." We may meet a woman on the job or through friends and see a "friend." Regardless of whether a man is a nerd who barely gets the time of day or a player who has to beat the women off of him, a man is looking for one thing: Ms. Right. Ms. Right is going to the woman who is physically appealing to the man as well as supportive emotionally. Let's look more closely at the emotional piece.

A man who has some level of character and a purpose in life wants sex from a woman. He's still human. This man, however, also wants an emotional connection. A man needs a woman he can talk to, share himself with, and also have physical gratification. He may not be thinking this way the first second he meets you but it will come up sooner or later depending on the man. With the more evolved man it will come up during the initial conversation. If you're not talking about anything special then your bomb body will not make any difference with certain men. I have had conversations with many men who, in describing a woman they just met, talked more about her personality than her body. That's when a woman has really made an impression on a man. Men want a woman they can talk to.

One issue I must address is the when some women act like a man should be interested in them because of their material possessions. Ladies, material goods don't sway a man to the extent you may think it does. A woman having a slamming job, nice place, car, and gold credit cards mean nothing if the man has those things as well. Despite this there is still a tiny minority of men interested in a woman's possessions. These will be the men who need a place to stay or a car to drive. Another group of men may care about a woman's possessions but that is only in terms of status. These are typically professional types who feel the need to impress the members of their social circle. Even in these cases the man will probably be more concerned about the woman's physical appearance than her personality traits.

I want to address the issue of "trophy wives." There are some men who want a beautiful woman on their arm and that's it. Most men, however, want a real woman on their arms. Ms. Right is more than a pretty face. Ms. Right will be beautiful with a nice body but will also have the emotional/spiritual traits the man finds attractive.

I have talked with many women who have expressed dislike over men choosing women who appear to be trophies. One thing women need to do is stop making those assumptions unless she specifically knows that a particular woman is a trophy. In my personal experience I have dated several women who have either been beauty contestants, or models. The LEAST formally educated of these women had a college degree and most of them had good common sense. My point is not to make assumptions. If you see a man with a "trophy" woman, simply move on because he is taken.

Ladies, I promised in the introduction that that I would share a powerful secret with you that would have men beating down your door. I gave subtle hints about the secret throughout this text but I'll share it with you now. Ladies, learn how to make love to a man's mind. The same way a man makes love to you by stimulating you physically a woman needs to learn how to stimulate a man mentally. Most men have a vast reserve of creativity which is untapped. A great secret of nature is that men need women to stimulate their creativity. Just like a woman is stimulated and impregnated by a man to create a baby, a man is the same way. Only men create with their minds. Men will create great literature, art, poetry, political, socioeconomic, and even spiritual systems when stimulated by the right woman.

Making love to a man's mind takes several forms. One way is to simply stroke his ego. Make that man feel appreciated. Don't be dishonest with him but give credit where it's due. If you think he's handsome tell him. If he did something special let him know. Stroking his ego makes him feel good about himself.

Another way of making love to a man's mind is simply being able to have an intelligent conversation with him on a variety of subjects. Read up on different subjects. Become someone that the man can learn from. Learn how to be comfortable with letting a man express himself freely around you. You're making love to his mind if he becomes comfortable with speaking freely around you.

Simply listening to what a man has to say is making love to his mind. A man needs a woman who is going to listen to him. Too many women assume they know more than the men they meet or don't want to hear what he has to say. We have a lot on our minds. We look for a woman we can talk to. Men have a lot going on. We just might not talk to you about it. There are several reasons for this. One is that he might not be inclined to share his plans with a woman who is simply a sex partner. Another reason is that sometimes a woman may not seem as if she would be supportive of his plans. Using myself as an example, I remember when I decided to start writing. Three different women essentially laughed at me. Two of them said writers don't make that much money. A third who worked in the publishing industry did not offer any type of assistance. Since you are reading this I guess I got the last laugh.

Making love to a man's mind is simply believing in his dreams. Men are looking for somebody to believe in them before they become successful. Too many women want to jump on the bandwagon once a man becomes successful. Men are cognizant of this. We remember when you didn't give us any play. Don't jump on the bandwagon and think you are going to be anything other than a sex partner. Men want somebody who is going to go through thick and thin for him.

Support is very important for a man and it's not about financial support. Most men I know what to control their destiny. It's hard work doing this. The biggest single complaint I have heard from men is the trouble finding a woman who will truly support them. Too many women do not want to show any love until after the man succeeds. It might be too late then. Ladies, make love to his mind by providing emotional support as he works on his purpose.

The most powerful thing a woman can do is to touch a man emotionally. Many men are guarded but when you touch our emotions we know you got us hooked.

# Conclusion

Well, there you have it. One man's view on how women can find the Right Man for them. It's not easy. It's going to take some work but all things in life that are worthwhile comes from effort. People are doing two things in their lives. They are either growing or dying. They are either going forward or they are going backward. There is no such thing as staying still. A law of the universe is that movement is constant so if you are not moving forward you are moving backward.

I have encountered many beautiful, intelligent, thoughtful women who are suffering without a mate or with the wrong mate. My heart goes out to these women because it doesn't have to be that way. Every single woman looking for the Right Man can find that man. To do so however she needs to change her approach because apparently it isn't working. A definition of insanity is to do the same thing over and over again and expect a change. The key to change is within a woman and not outside of her. If a woman keeps running into knuckleheads, instead of complaining that all men are no good, she needs to ask herself why she keeps running into certain types of men.    It's not that all men are knuckleheads it's that she runs into the knuckleheads.    The woman who thinks that all men have a potential for greatness will run into these men.    A woman who believes men are cheaters will run into these men.    Do you, the woman reading this, get the idea?    You are the one creating the reality and if you want a change you have to change yourself.    To bring this full circle you have to believe that you can make the change.

Thank you for your time.

Peace,

# Rom Wills

# About the Author

Who is Rom Wills? I have had many words used to describe me. I've been called mysterious, brilliant, and goofy. I'm the type of person who can read a comic book in the morning and an obscure book on deep metaphysics in the evening. I can hang out on a street corner one moment and with powerful movers and shakers the next. I can talk about the read option offense in pro football and the inner workings of the national economy the next. I can say without conceit that I could star in some "Most Interesting Man in the World" commercials. I'm formally educated with advanced degrees and yet my best education has come from simply living life. There are very few things I haven't either personally experienced or know someone who has experienced certain things. My life would make a very compelling movie.

So who is Rom Wills? I'm a man who is on a mission to make a difference in the lives of the people I touch. Everything that I have experienced in life, good and bad, has been a life lesson. Through my writings, lectures, workshops, or talking trash in a barbershop I strive to share something that will positively impact the people around me.

Rom Wills is the author of the international bestseller Nice Guys and Players and the follow-up Sexual Chemistry.

Follow Rom on the World Wide Web:
www.romwills.com
Facebook.com/Willspublishing
Twitter: @RomWills1